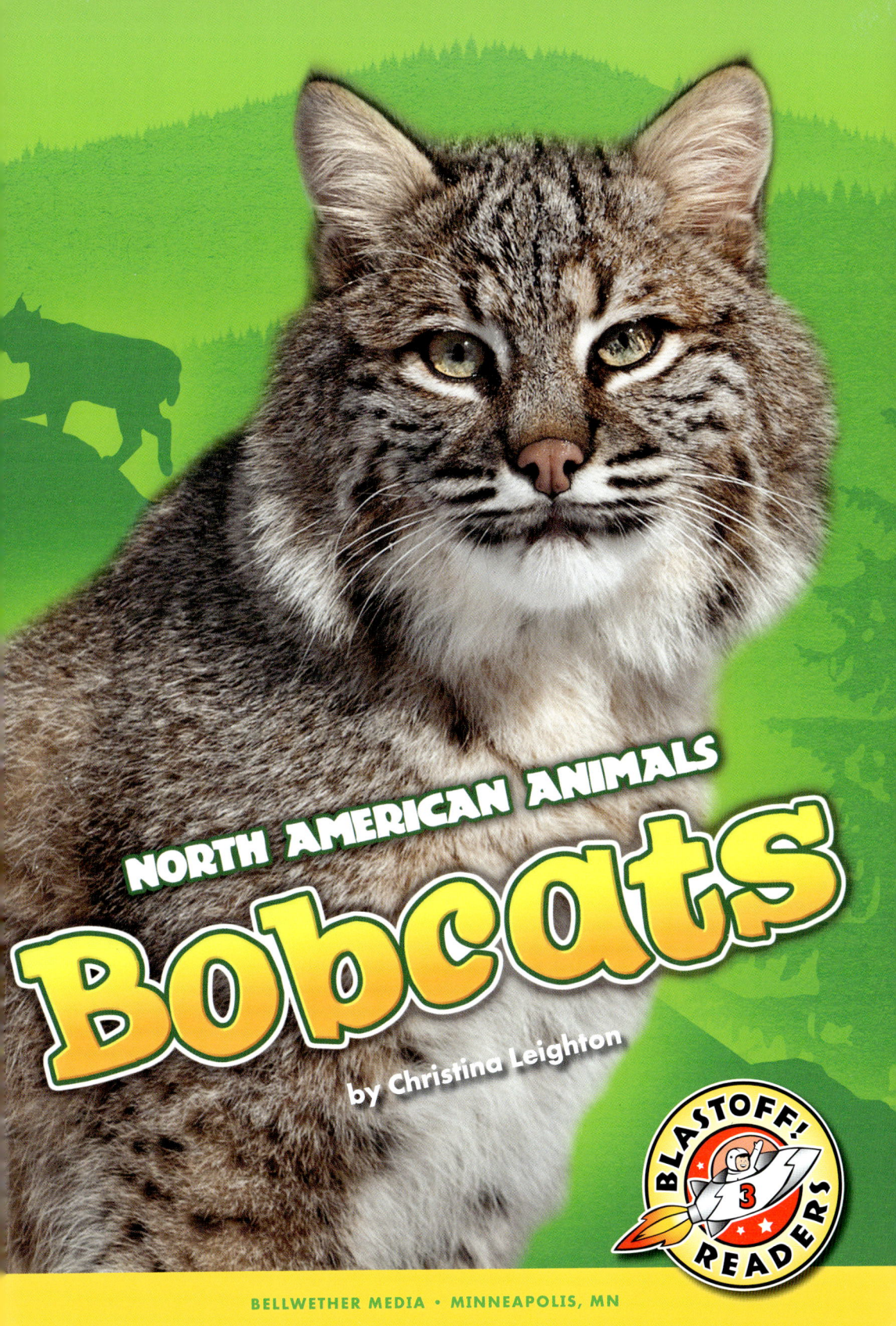

NORTH AMERICAN ANIMALS
Bobcats

by Christina Leighton

Note to Librarians, Teachers, and Parents:

Blastoff! Readers are carefully developed by literacy experts and combine standards-based content with developmentally appropriate text.

Level 1 provides the most support through repetition of high-frequency words, light text, predictable sentence patterns, and strong visual support.

Level 2 offers early readers a bit more challenge through varied simple sentences, increased text load, and less repetition of high-frequency words.

Level 3 advances early-fluent readers toward fluency through increased text and concept load, less reliance on visuals, longer sentences, and more literary language.

Level 4 builds reading stamina by providing more text per page, increased use of punctuation, greater variation in sentence patterns, and increasingly challenging vocabulary.

Level 5 encourages children to move from "learning to read" to "reading to learn" by providing even more text, varied writing styles, and less familiar topics.

Whichever book is right for your reader, Blastoff! Readers are the perfect books to build confidence and encourage a love of reading that will last a lifetime!

This edition first published in 2017 by Bellwether Media, Inc.

No part of this publication may be reproduced in whole or in part without written permission of the publisher. For information regarding permission, write to Bellwether Media, Inc., Attention: Permissions Department, 5357 Penn Avenue South, Minneapolis, MN 55419.

Library of Congress Cataloging-in-Publication Data
Names: Leighton, Christina, author.
Title: Bobcats / by Christina Leighton.
Other titles: Blastoff! Readers. 3, North American Animals.
Description: Minneapolis, MN : Bellwether Media, Inc., 2017. | Series: Blastoff! Readers. North American Animals | Audience: Ages 5-8. | Audience: K to grade 3. | Includes bibliographical references and index.
Identifiers: LCCN 2016032041 (print) | LCCN 2016038407 (ebook) | ISBN 9781626175655 (hardcover : alk. paper) | ISBN 9781681032863 (ebook)
Subjects: LCSH: Bobcat–Juvenile literature.
Classification: LCC QL737.C23 L444 2017 (print) | LCC QL737.C23 (ebook) | DDC 599.75/36–dc23
LC record available at https://lccn.loc.gov/2016032041

Editor: Betsy Rathburn   Designer: Brittany McIntosh

Text copyright © 2017 by Bellwether Media, Inc. BLASTOFF! READERS and associated logos are trademarks and/or registered trademarks of Bellwether Media, Inc. SCHOLASTIC, CHILDREN'S PRESS, and associated logos are trademarks and/or registered trademarks of Scholastic Inc.

Printed in the United States of America, North Mankato, MN.

Table of Contents

What Are Bobcats?	4
Bobbed Bottoms	8
Pouncing on Prey	12
Baby Bobcats	18
Glossary	22
To Learn More	23
Index	24

What Are Bobcats?

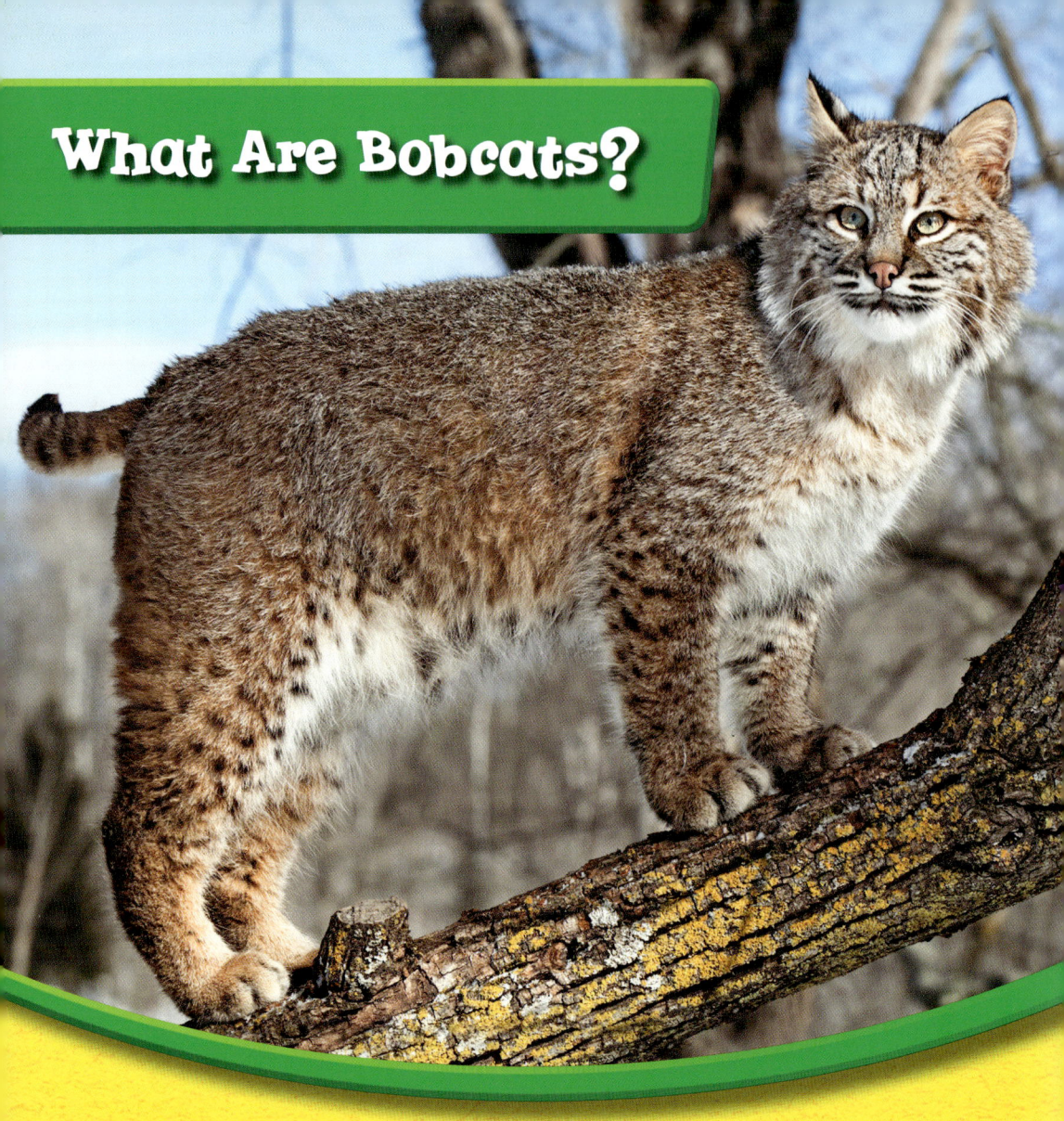

Bobcats are **mammals** that live across North America. Their range stretches from southern Canada to Mexico.

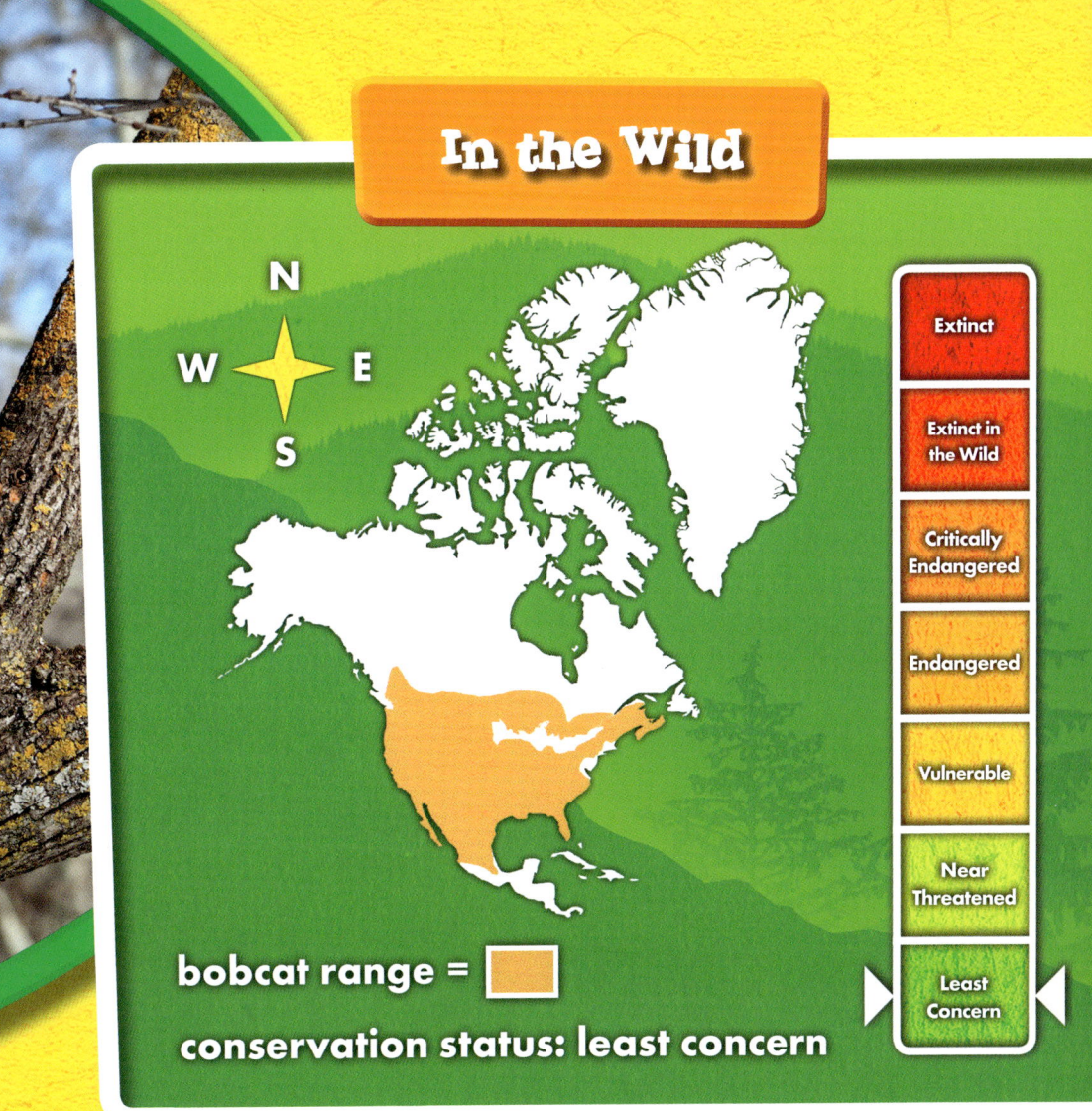

Their range in North America is the widest of any **native** cat.

Bobcats are found in many **habitats**. They **adapt** well to different places.

Some bobcats prowl deserts. Others roam mountainsides. They also live in forests and swamps.

Bobbed Bottoms

Bobcats are medium-sized wildcats. They are about two times bigger than common house cats.

Their bodies are between 26 and 41 inches (66 and 104 centimeters) long. They weigh up to 30 pounds (14 kilograms).

Identify a Bobcat

bobbed tail   dark spots   ruff

Bobcats are named for their **bobbed** tails. They have reddish brown coats with dark spots and stripes.

Short **ear tufts** top their ears. **Ruffs** grow on the sides of their faces.

← ear tuft

Pouncing on Prey

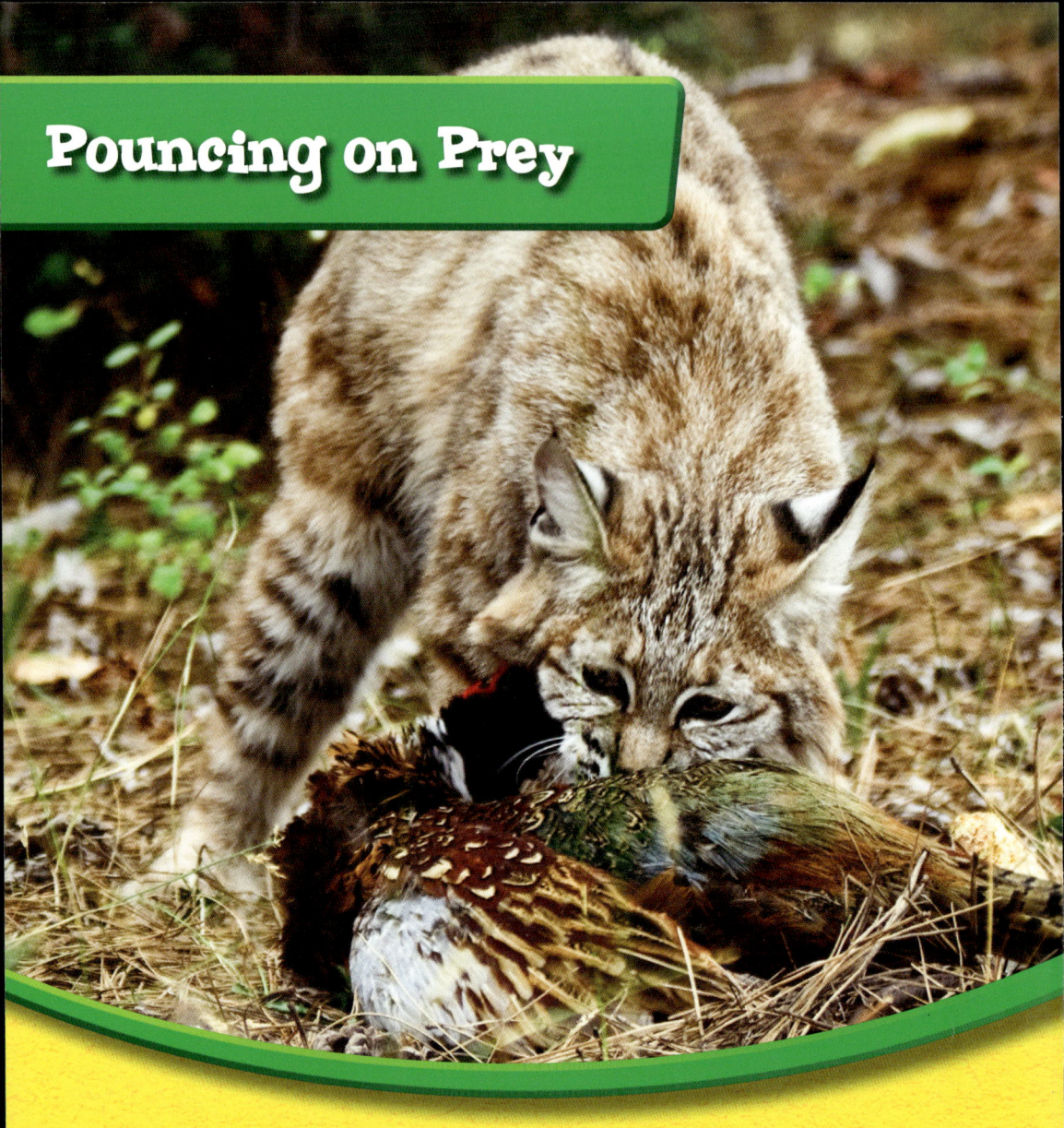

Bobcats are **carnivores** with excellent eyesight and hearing. These help them spot **prey** in the dark.

On the Menu

collared lizards

deer mice

cottontail rabbits

gray squirrels

white-tailed deer

ring-necked pheasants

Rabbits, squirrels, and mice are favorite meals. Bobcats can also take down deer.

These wildcats use their sharp claws to climb trees and grab food. Their long, powerful legs also help them hunt.

They run up to 30 miles (48 kilometers) per hour. They can leap on prey from 12 feet (3.7 meters) away!

Bobcats like to surprise their prey. These **stealthy** hunters first wait in bushes or rocky areas for food to arrive.

Then they sneak up from behind. When the time is right, they **pounce**!

Baby Bobcats

Female bobcats look for **dens** in spring. There, they give birth to baby bobcats. The **kittens** open their eyes after ten days.

Baby Facts

Name for babies:	kittens
Size of litter:	1 to 6 kittens
Length of pregnancy:	2 months
Time spent with mom:	8 months

The kittens **nurse** for about two months. Then their mother teaches them to find food.

In less than one year, they are ready to hunt on their own!

Glossary

adapt—to become comfortable with something

bobbed—short and rounded

carnivores—animals that only eat meat

dens—sheltered places; bobcats make dens underground, under rocks, or in hollow trees.

ear tufts—fur on top of bobcat ears that grows close together

habitats—lands with certain types of plants, animals, and weather

kittens—baby bobcats

mammals—warm-blooded animals that have backbones and feed their young milk

native—originally from a certain place

nurse—to drink mom's milk

pounce—to suddenly jump on something to catch it

prey—animals that are hunted by other animals for food

ruffs—long fur that hangs down

stealthy—quiet and secret

To Learn More

AT THE LIBRARY
Goldish, Meish. *Bobcat*. New York, N.Y.: Bearport Publishing, 2015.

Grucella, Ann. *Bobcats*. New York, N.Y.: Gareth Stevens Pub., 2013.

Randall, Henry. *Bobcats*. New York, N.Y.: PowerKids Press, 2011.

ON THE WEB
Learning more about bobcats is as easy as 1, 2, 3.

1. Go to www.factsurfer.com.
2. Enter "bobcats" into the search box.
3. Click the "Surf" button and you will see a list of related web sites.

With factsurfer.com, finding more information is just a click away.

Index

bodies, 9
Canada, 4
carnivores, 12
claws, 14
climb, 14
coats, 10
dens, 18
deserts, 7
ear tufts, 11
eyesight, 12
females, 18
food, 14, 16, 20
forests, 7
habitats, 6
hearing, 12
hunt, 14, 21
kittens, 18, 19, 20
leap, 15
legs, 14
mammals, 4

Mexico, 4
mountainsides, 7
nurse, 20
pounce, 17
prey, 12, 13, 15, 16
range, 4, 5
ruffs, 10, 11
run, 15
seasons, 18
size, 8, 9
sneak, 17
swamps, 7
tails, 10

The images in this book are reproduced through the courtesy of: Geoffrey Kuchera, front cover, pp. 4, 14, 21; Robynrg, pp. 6, 16; Rinus Baak, p. 7; K. Wothe/ picture alliance/ blickwinkel/ K/ Newscom, p. 8; visceralimage, p. 10 (top left); MelaniWright, p. 10 (top center); Holly Kuchera, p. 10 (top right); Steven Frame, p. 10 (bottom); Volodymyr Burdiak, p. 11; Rick Dalton - Wildlife/ Alamy Stock Photo, p. 12; Matt Jeppson, p. 13 (top left); Close Encounters Photo, p. 13 (top right); Michael Chatt, p. 13 (center left); Michael Rowlandson, p. 13 (center right); JAMES PIERCE, p. 13 (bottom left); Robert L Kothenbeutel, p. 13 (bottom right); Superstock/ Glow Images, p. 15; Don Johnston/ Age Fotostock, p. 17; Minden Pictures/ Minden Pictures/ SuperStock, p. 18; critterbiz, p. 19; Illg, Gordon & Cathy/ Animals Animals, p. 20.